Welcome to a walk through Wenatchee, Washington. In this book I was looking to show a glimpse of the town I live in. The work contained within is the product of various walks through the town from 2009 to 2015. All images are the property of Corey Oakes and any applicable permission has been gained prior to publishing of this work. If there are any concerns over any of the information, or images contained in this volume, please contact Corey Oakes immediately at;

Corey Oakes

corey-oakes@hotmail.com

You may also contact him via the Author Central Page on Amazon.com.

Once in a while you find time to take a walk and you find beauty everywhere you look. Causing you to wonder, why you never noticed it before. This was especially true for me, considering it was the beauty in the town where I live. So I decided to collect these walks in images that I could share with others who may be in need of seeing the beauty in their towns.

When I decided to start this project in the summer of 2009 I wasn't really sure where it was going to go. In fact, I only came to the conclusion that it would be a walk through Wenatchee recently. When I did find my inspiration for the final project, I decided to compile pieces of my favorite walks to complete a walk for those who aren't from here. Not one of those tourist walks where you only see the market or the historic museum, but a walk through town as one of the locals would take. I hope you will enjoy this stroll through Wenatchee with me and maybe even feel inspired to explore it for yourself. -Corey Oakes

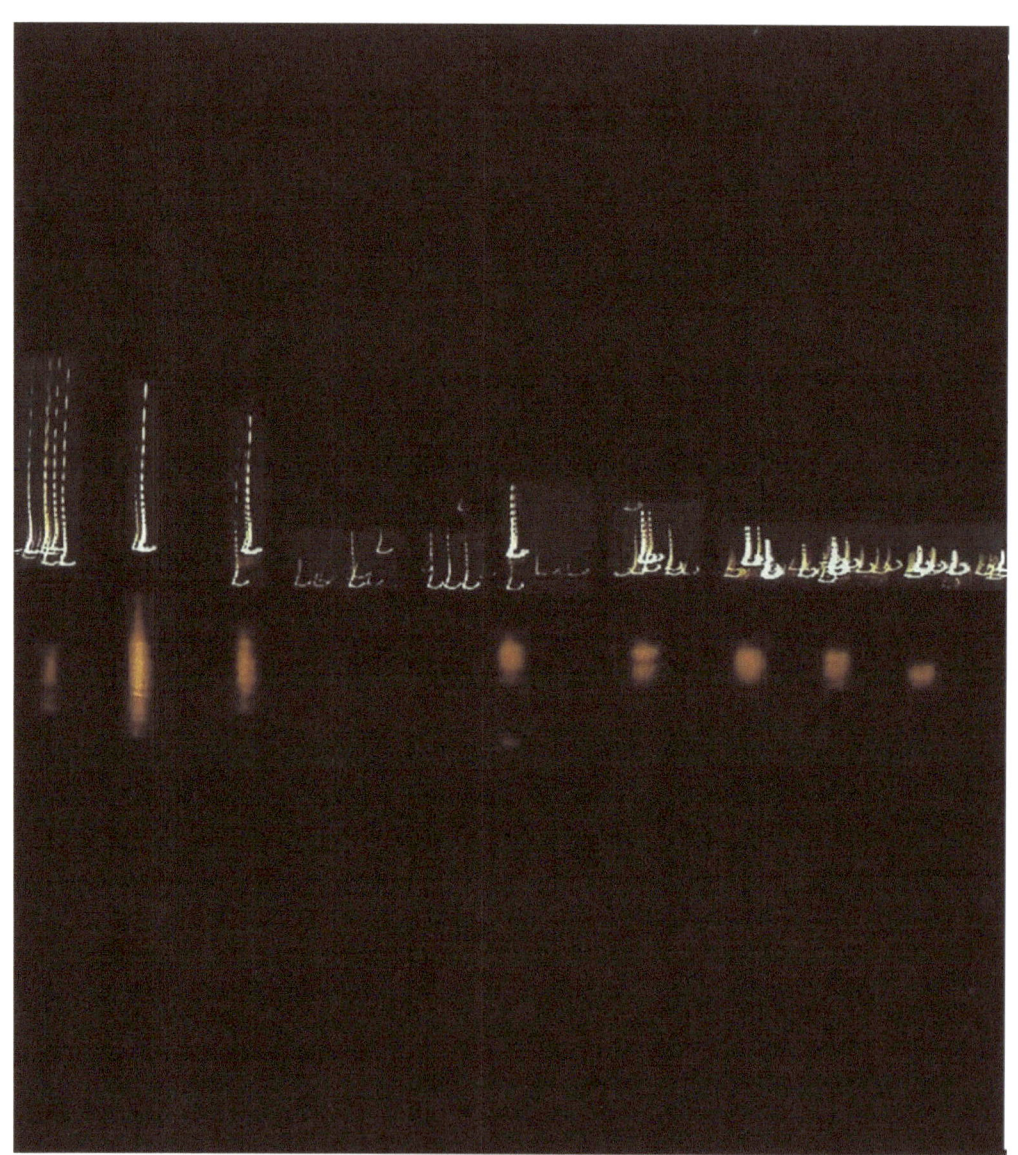

"Wenatchee" 2009

Wenatchee, Washington is a city located in the center of the state, with the mighty Columbia River separating the two cities which make up the greater Wenatchee area. It is a center for agriculture, mainly fruits and wines. It is a high desert landscape surrounded by picturesque mountains. They have a huge amount of outdoor activities such as, hiking, swimming, rafting, skiing, biking and even airplanes, go carts and racing. In fact one would be very hard pressed to find an outdoor activity which is not offered in some form here. The weather is beautiful as well, with most of the year being sunny. The arts are also very well represented here, with programs like arts on the avenues and a thriving set of impromptu gallery spaces throughout the downtown corridor. There are artist designed bridges that allow you to cross from the city center over the railroad to the thriving waterfront. With many eclectic and ever-changing art installations, you will never see the same thing for too long. The town which used to only be known for Apple Blossom and the apple industry has really begun to come into its own in the last six years and even I find it hard to see everything before it is ultimately changed.

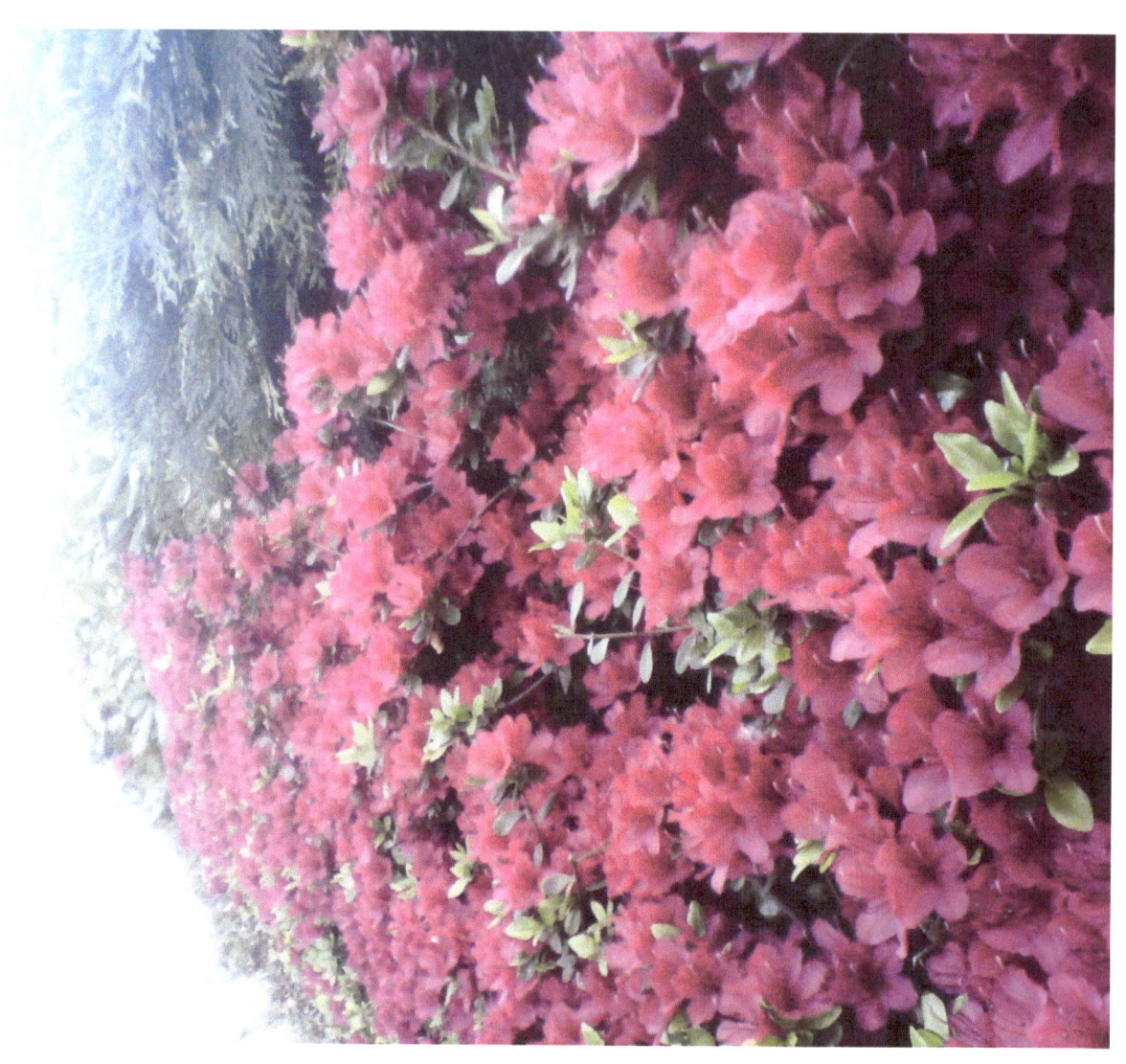

"Wall of Rhody's" 2015

So let us begin our walk at the corner of Fifth Street and Miller. Here as we stroll toward Miller Street we are greeted by radiant bright pink Rhododendrons, which create a wall of fragrance. This mixes with the almost overwhelmingly bright glow of the ethereal wall of pink. The wall is about fifteen feet to the corner of the intersection and is mixed with weeping cedar, which on a nice day creates a burst of scents. With the sun shining down like a warm blanket and a slight breeze caressing your face, spreading a happy warm feeling to carry us forward. This is a great way to begin, as we can carry the beauty of the rhody's with us as we traverse our way to Cherry Street. As we carry with us, this great burst of beauty created by some landscaping genius to begin this walk to experience all of the images and senses that Wenatchee has to offer.

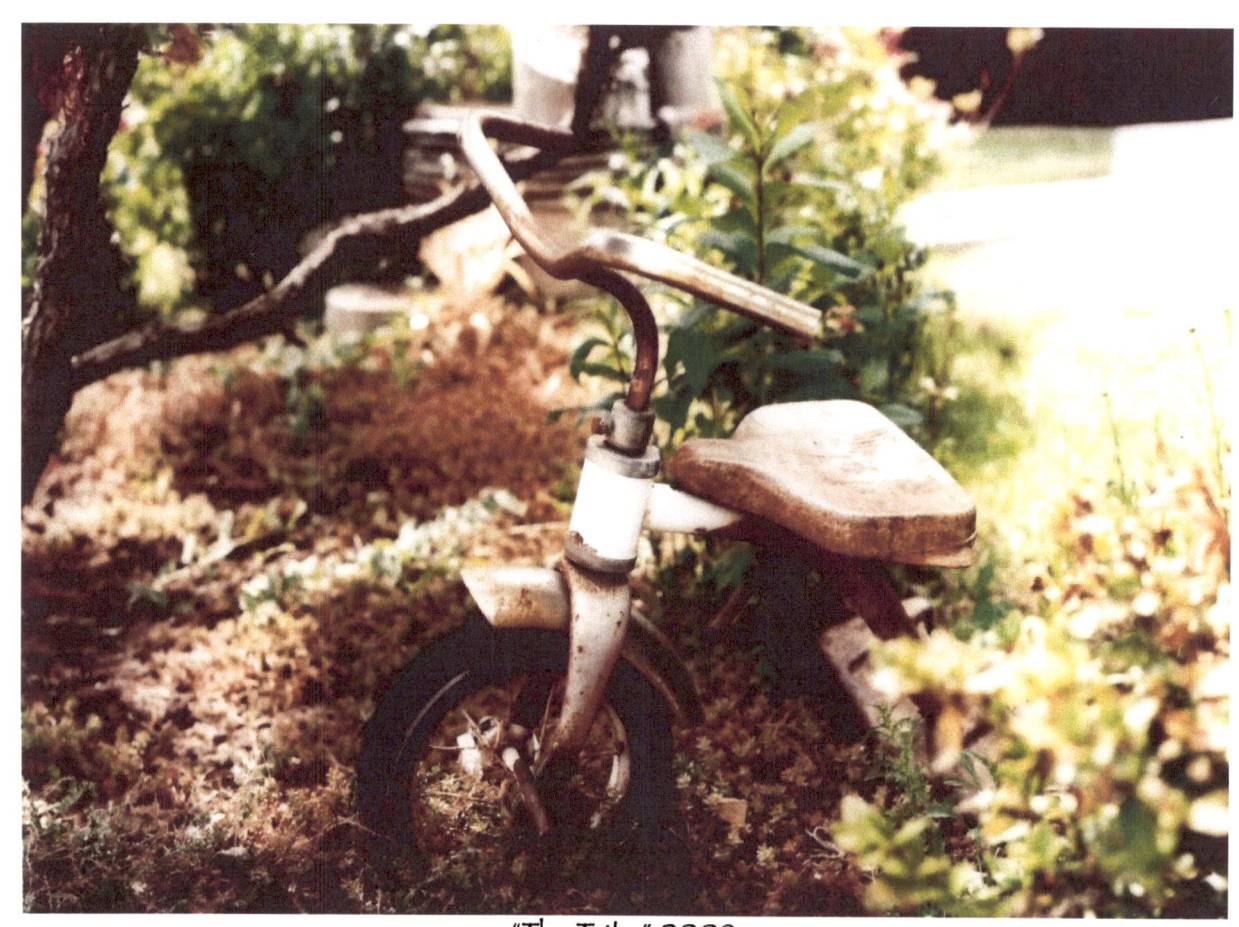

"The Trike" 2009

As we continue our stroll, we head south on Miller toward Cherry Street. Along the way there are a great many unique houses, as well as historical homes. All of which are architectural beauties. One is a stone cottage looking home with lots of landscaped spaces. Others are reminiscent of southwestern styles, with curved driveways and columned entryways. Each with a style all their own much like Wenatchee itself. As you near the corner of Cherry, you find a service station slash ice cream slash coffee place, Just another example of Wenatchee ingenuity. Passing the expansive baseball and soccer fields of the middle school, the shape of which is more like a windblown snow drift than a middle school. We make our way left down Cherry Street and we come to Alaska Avenue, where we will be making our way right down one of the older areas of town. Now many of the homes in the area are not really considered the best in the area, but I would challenge you to look a little deeper, as many of these homes have some of the most unique landscaping that I have seen. Along the way there are field of sunflowers, baskets made of bushes and most interesting to me was a lonely little tricycle. There sitting tucked under a protective Japanese maple sat this iconic image of childhood, seemingly waiting for the next generation of curious children to dare each other to ride it. Yet it fit in with the rustic demeanor of the landscape, tying together imaginative uses of various archaic drinking vessels and more traditional well-kept landscaping designs. It has become one of my most loved photos over the years, maybe due to its ability to remind me of my childhood.

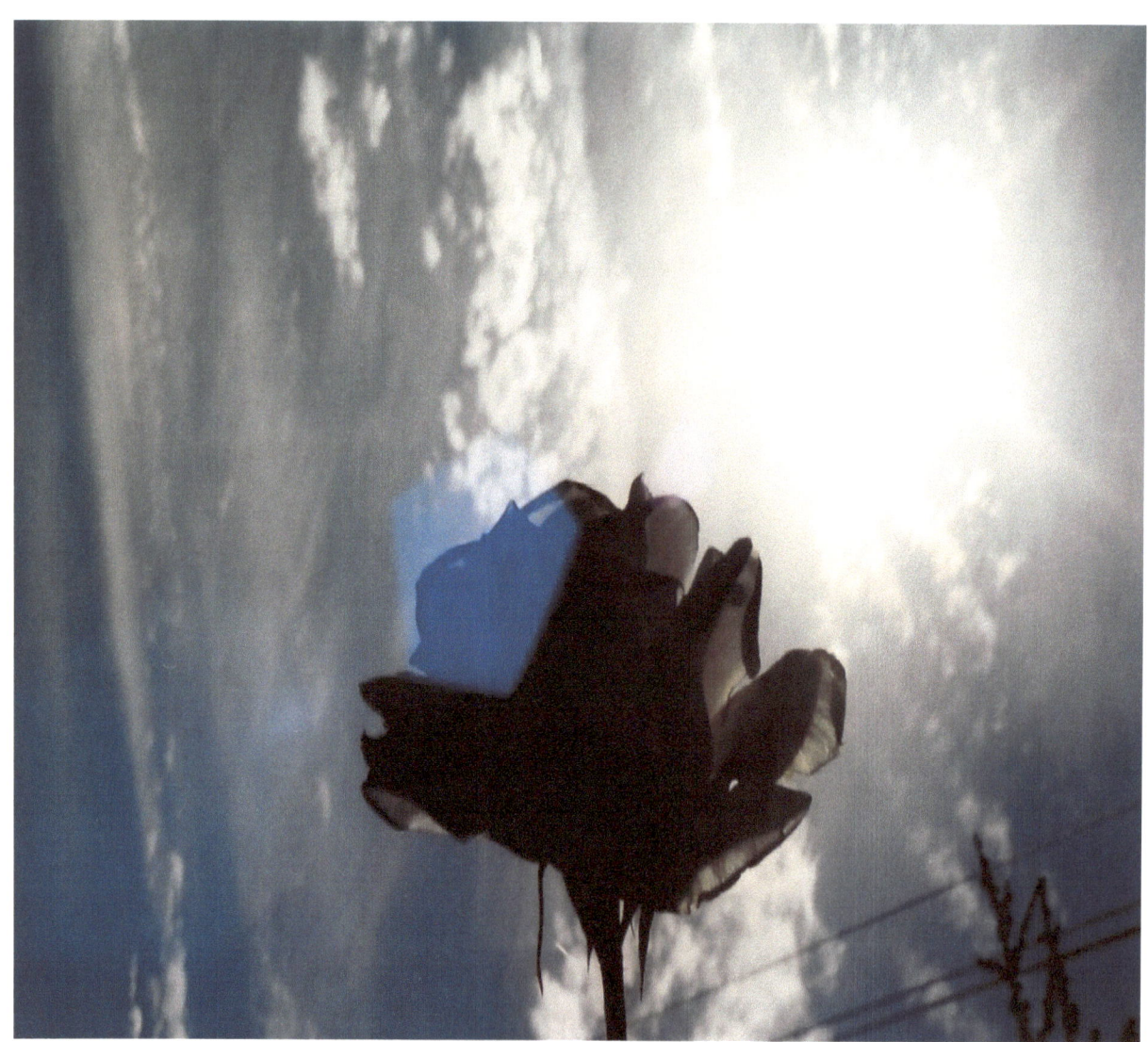

"Blue Rose "2009

Now our journey takes a bit of a twist, as we head farther south toward Saddle Rock. As we make our way through the maze of twisty residential streets from Alaska to Ferry Street and up to Red Apple Rd. We will pass a hospital and begin to see the mountains growing closer to our right. Standing above this view are two imposing looking rock formations, which seem to look as if some giant had thrown his saddle over the tops of the rolling hills in an attempt to ride the mountains. We may never know why this mythical giant left his saddle here, but it certainly seems worthy of a hike to see if we can ride the mountains too. Along the way up Red Apple Road and left back on to Miller Avenue, we encounter a single white rose stretched far out over the sidewalk. In the blazing afternoon sun, it is transformed into a brilliant unique blue rose, yearning to escape from the confines of the fence meant to keep it. I still can see that yearning in the photo today, as if it were still trying to reach the sun.

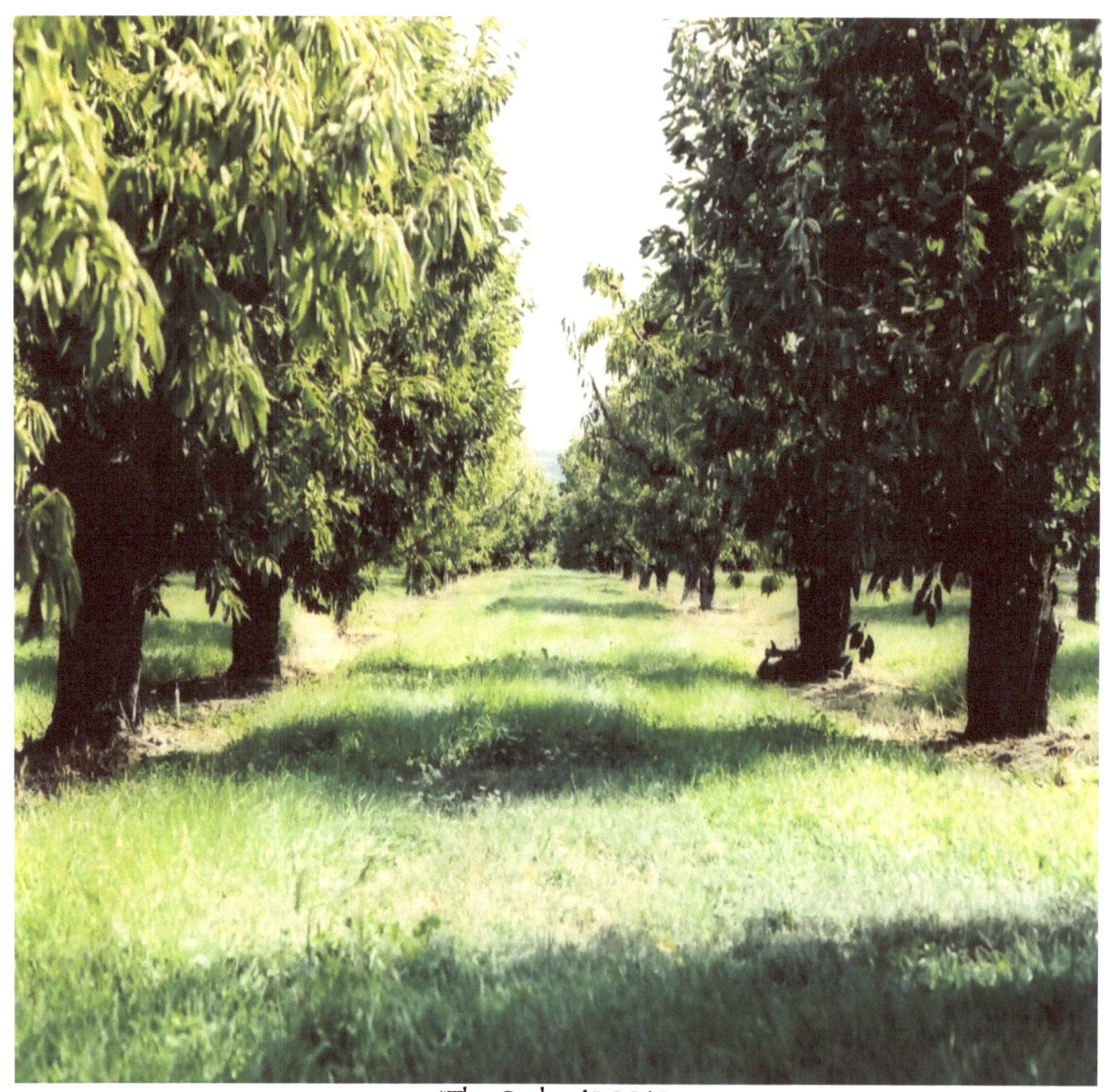

"The Orchard" 2010

As we are making our way towards the saddled mountains, it begins to dawn on us just how hot this walk has become. Luckily for us right across the street is an orchard in the full throws of spring. In its cool embrace, we rest taking in the cool caress of the orchard grass. As we listen to the whispers of the wind through the musical boughs of the trees.

Sitting here in this shaded oasis amongst the heat of the noon day sun, I am also reminded of the Johnny Appleseed stories from my childhood. Imagining what it would be like to be that carefree youth traveling around the countryside spreading seeds that will bear fruit. Oh if only this were life, eh? No cares about having enough of something, or being able to put a roof over one's head, just traveling and enjoying life. Yet, as we wake from our mid days dream, we are reminded of the carefree moment that we have just experienced. Now we are ready to dare to saddle a mountain, so it's on to Saddle Rock we go!

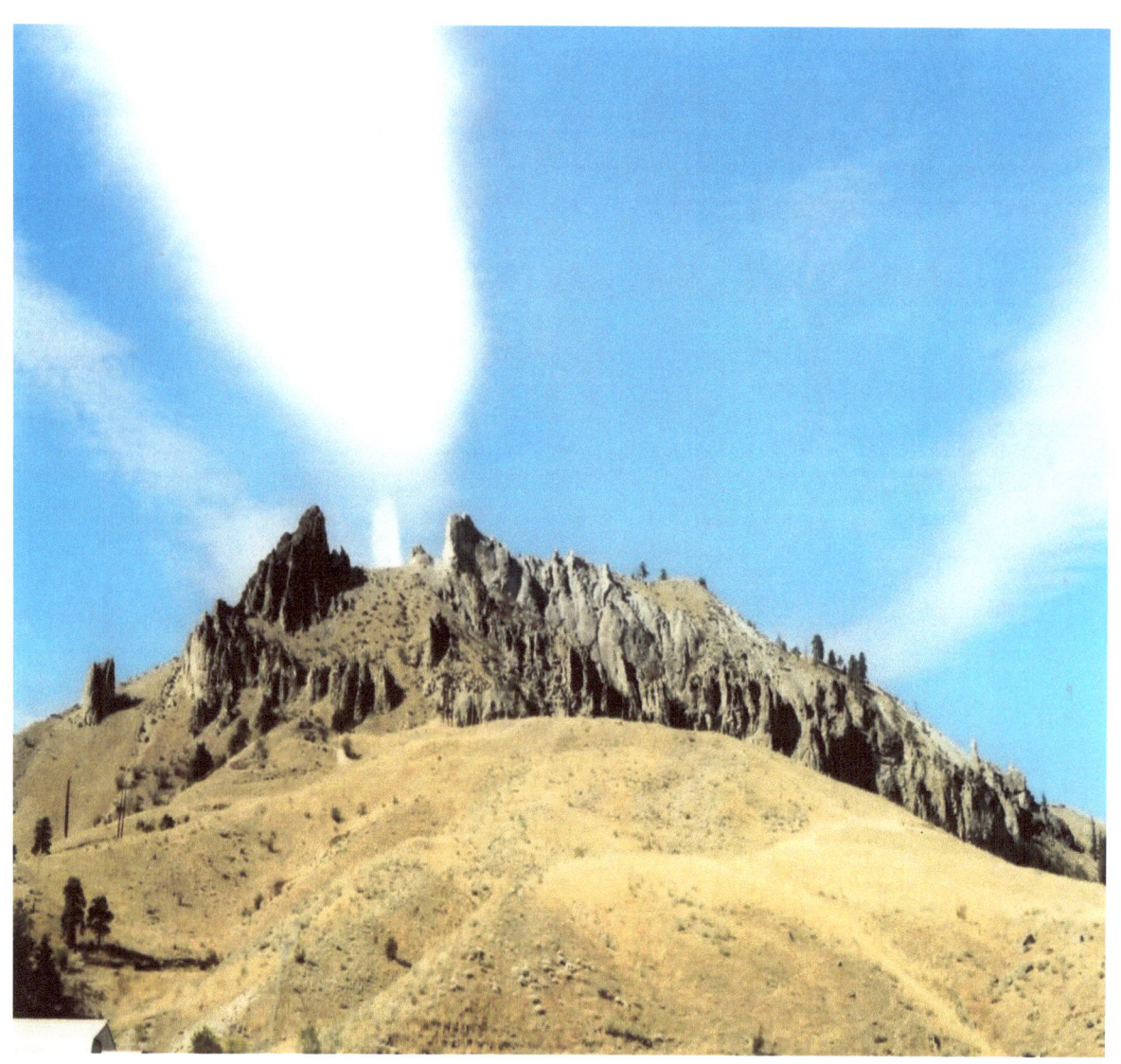

"Saddle Rock" 2010

As we rise from our surprisingly restful time in the cool orchard, we can see the imposing rock saddle above us, seeming much bigger than before. As we traverse the road that seems to go right up the hill, we are surprised to find a horse riding association on the right. The Appleatchee Riders, which has been in the valley for many years. The Saddle Rock area is conserved by many groups, but the Appleatchee are largely responsible for the way the large gulch next to it looks today. We will save that trip for another time. Ascending the trail, we gaze up at the rock formations which seem to reach to the sky. There are a few choice trails which will bring us to the saddle, but we will choose the easier road in the middle. The trail winds around smaller outcroppings which have rest spots that give us different vantage points to view the city from. As we ascend further towards our goal of the saddle, we must also remember to keep an ear out for the native occupants of this park, the rattle snake. With the sun beating down upon us, we trek on, up the winding road, which seems to wash out from time to time. About two thirds of the way up, we reach the end of the road, which harbors an oasis of shade where we can rest before the steep climb up the slippery shale that continues to the saddle itself.

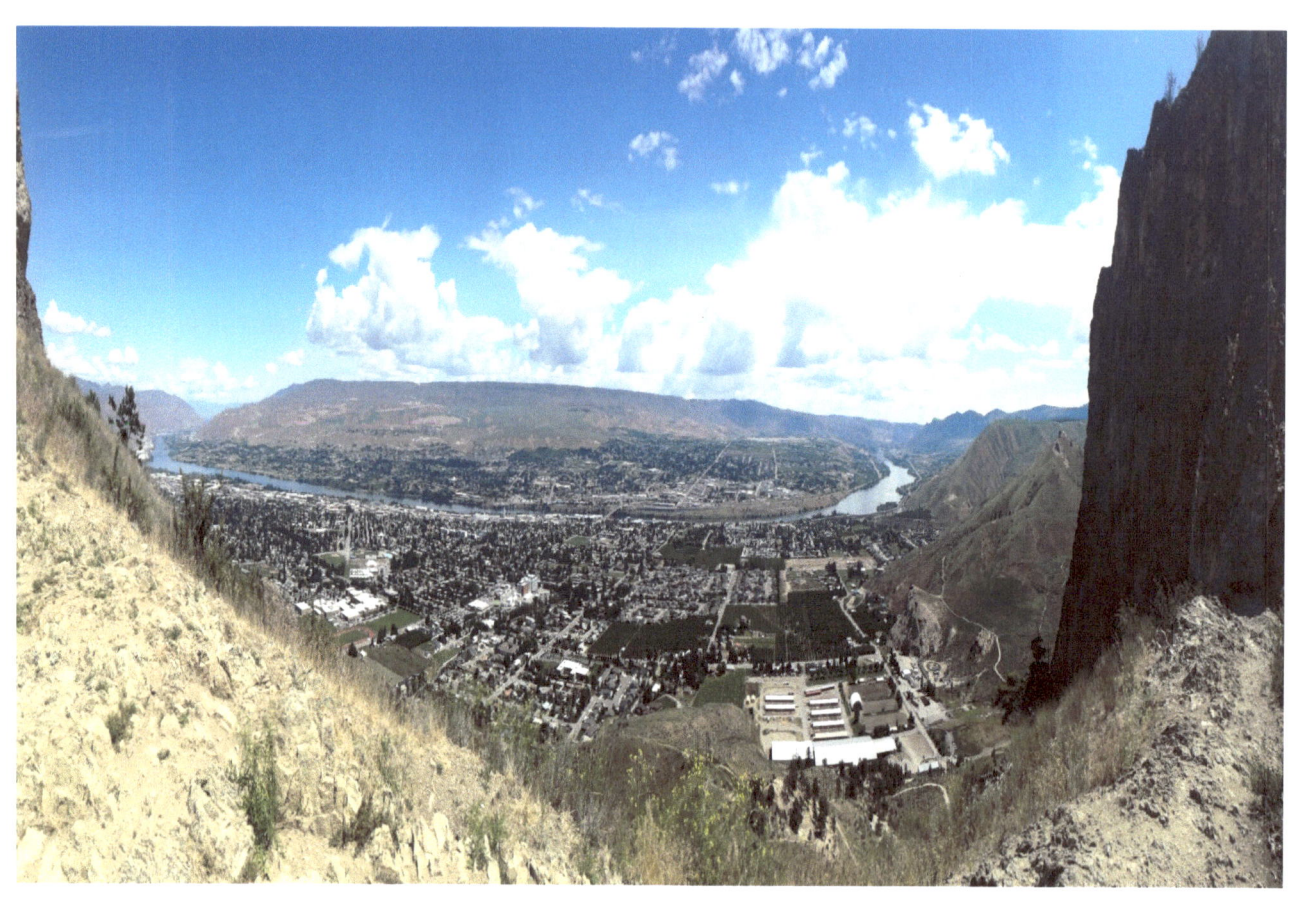

"Valley from the Saddle" 2015

As we rise from our rest under the desert oasis, we must fight to ascend the final stretch to the saddle and the wonderful view that it affords us. Once we arrive, we are greeted with both the relief that we have finally reached the top, as well as a glorious panoramic view of the valley below. Two rivers meet at the north end and the south winds like a snake through the ascending canyon walls. After a much deserved rest, we begin our ascent down the back side of the saddle and back down the now familiar road to the waiting oasis at the bottom. As we make our way, we are greeted by wildflowers and colorful rocks, which have made their own journey from the top. The smells of this grassy place seem to linger with us a bit longer on this trip down. Maybe it's just because were going down the hill and not fighting our way up the hot hillside. In fact even the sun feels a bit less intense, or maybe it too is making its downward journey from the top.

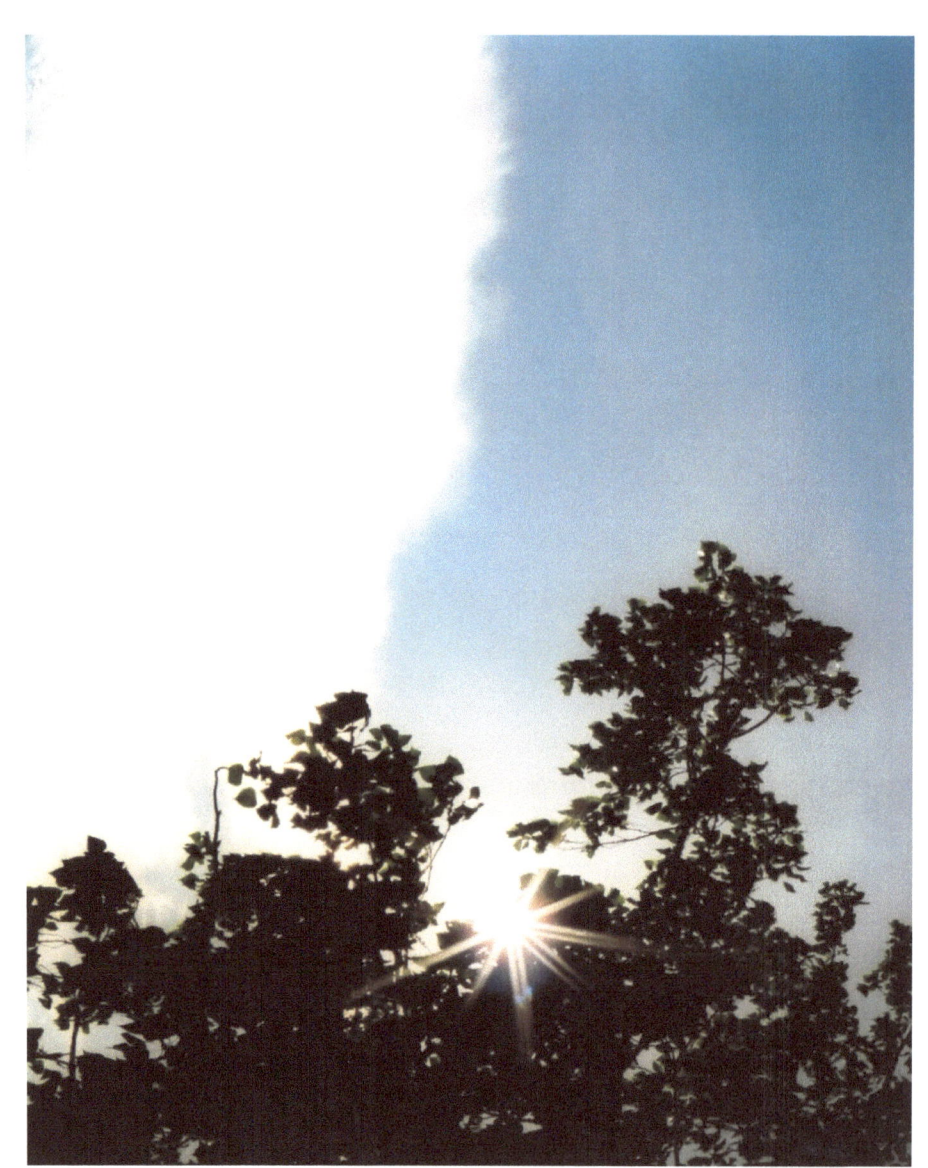

"Split Sky" 2009

This second oasis at the parking lot at the bottom seems to bring us to a wonderful end to our journey to the saddled mountain of the giants. Here the world seems to stop to let us admire it, with the clouds parting just right to allow us a perfect view of the beauty which is contained within the branches of the tree. With the sun just peeking through to remind us that it waits for us to emerge from our cooling refuge. Here we will decide on our next leg of this journey. Through much deliberation and the slow ending of the day approaching, we decide on following our path backwards toward Miller and Orondo Streets. This will afford us a mostly downhill journey to the waterfront. Rising from our deliberation, we begin the trek back down past the Appleatchee Riders and around the bend to Miller Street. From here we follow the familiar path to the corner gas station on Orondo Street. The station offers some of the best ice cream in the valley and is always occupied by friendly, helpful staff. After sampling our cold treats, we follow the winding road down toward the historic courthouse and Memorial Park. There is a rose garden next to the courthouse here, which in the spring blooms a beautiful blanket of colors and aromas that brings a certain pep back into your step. Here we will continue down Orondo Street towards Wenatchee Avenue.

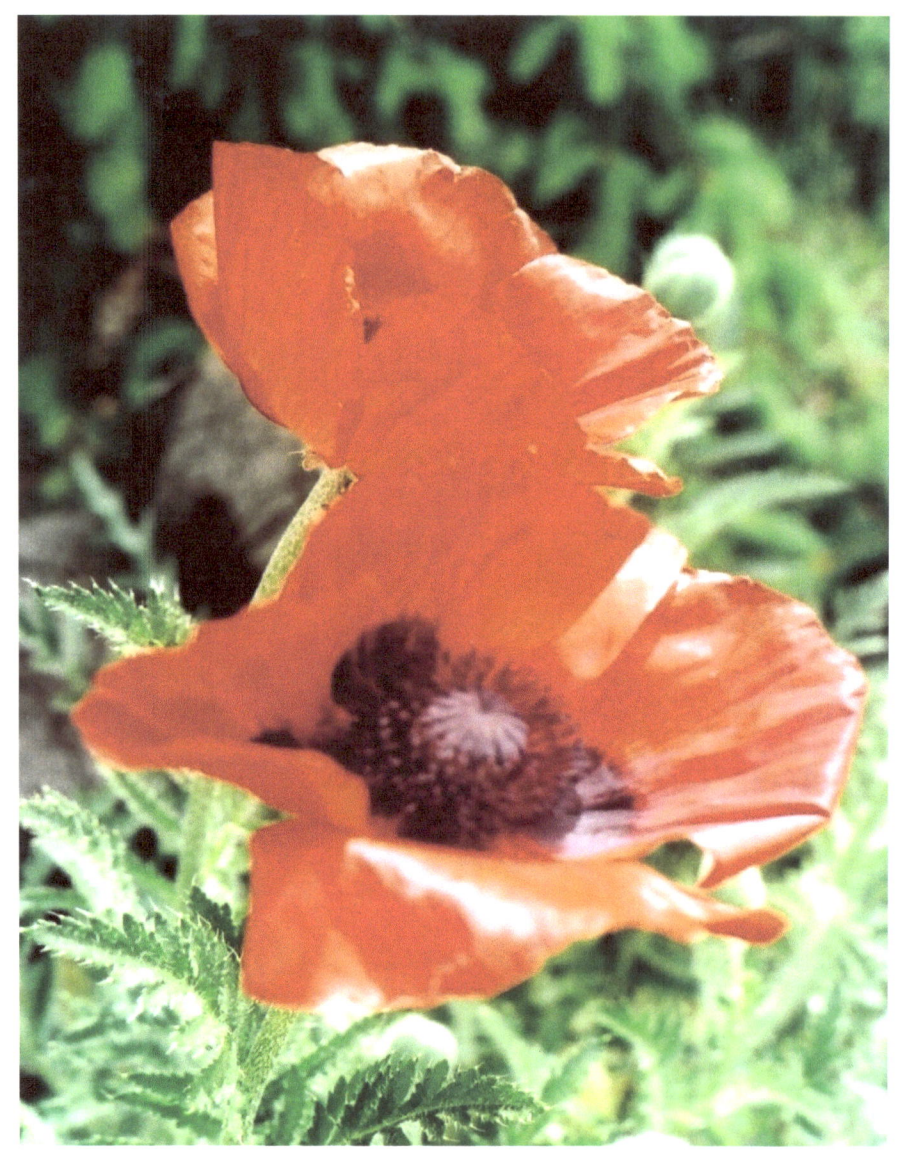

"Poppy's" 2013

. At the bottom of the park, we find a beautiful red poppy clinging to life on the sidewalk. Stopping to take the picture, I am struck by the fragility of the life that I am trying to capture. As if somehow this poppy's tragic story is somehow a part of my own. Which in some grand Buddhist way, it is. Therefore, I am glad that I was able to capture its lovely image before it was wiped out by a well-meaning gardener. While we are pondering the fragile life of the poppy, we are beginning to realize the late hour and try to resume our journey, leaving our pondering of poppies for another day. Making our way down the road, we notice that the road itself has changed. Here are the last remnants of another time in the city's history, the brick road. This remnant could have easily been covered in the more familiar blacktop, but the people here find a certain comfort in their visible history, so here it remains for all future generations to enjoy. Acting as a constant reminder of our recent past, where the road was shared by horses and wagons.

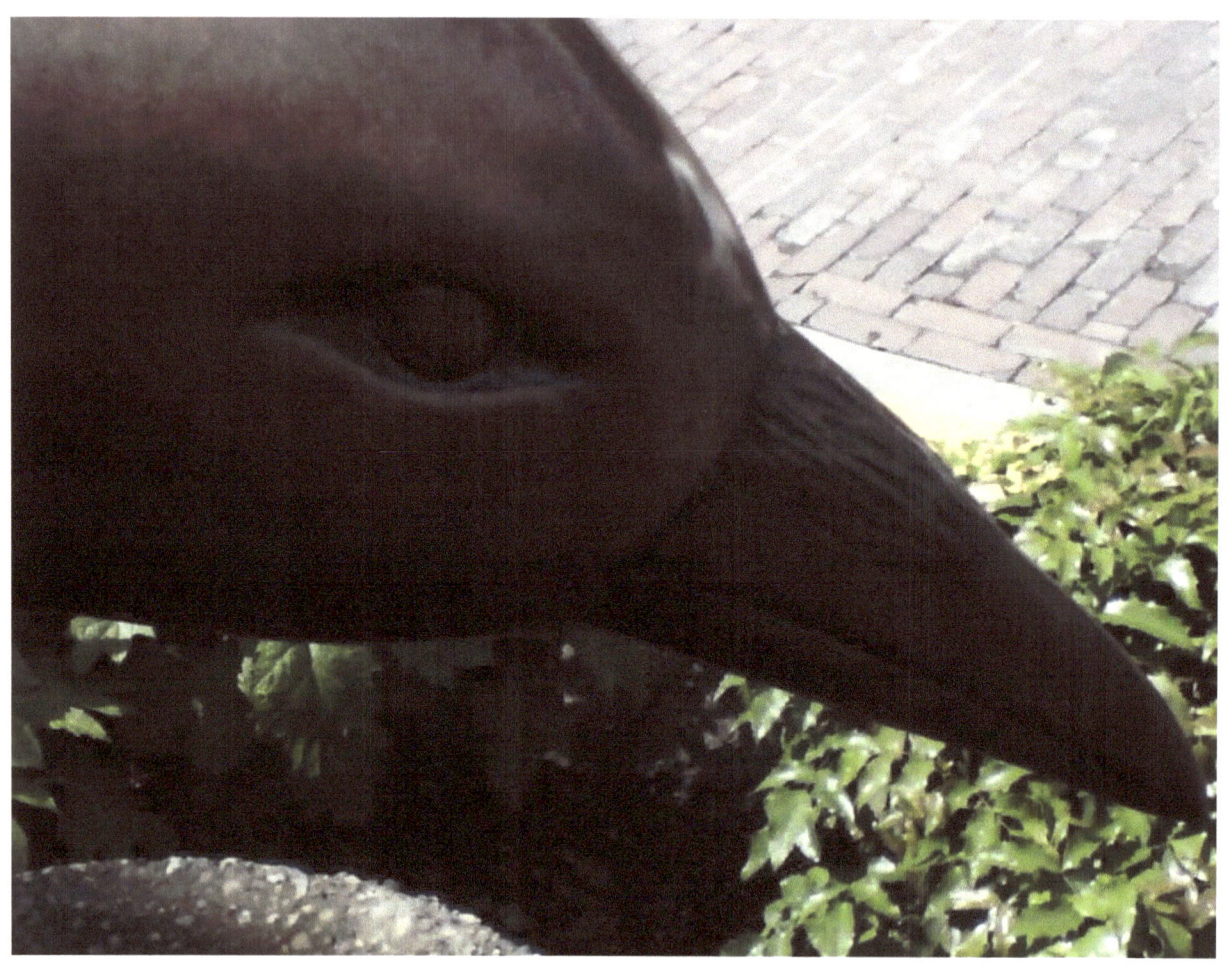

"Bowed Raven" by: Georgia Gerber

Following this red brick road, we at last reach Wenatchee Avenue, where we are greeted with a sculpture from the Art on the Avenues exhibit, a bowing raven. How fitting as it seems to bow to show us the way on our journey through its home. With a smiling beak and a trickster look to his eyes, he seems to point us in the direction of the Pybus Market and the waterfront. Surrounded by this beckoning art and the nostalgic brick street, we are struck that it seems different here on the Avenue. It is almost like a different town, with an inviting main street, riddled with charm. It beckons us to come and see what it has to offer. So, as we thank our brass guide, we move toward the beckoning of our inner shopper and decide to deviate from our more direct path to the Pybus Market and travel the nostalgic Avenue. Down the block a bit there is what looks to be a four sided antique clock with the gears easily visible. Another piece of the long ago from Wenatchee's past.

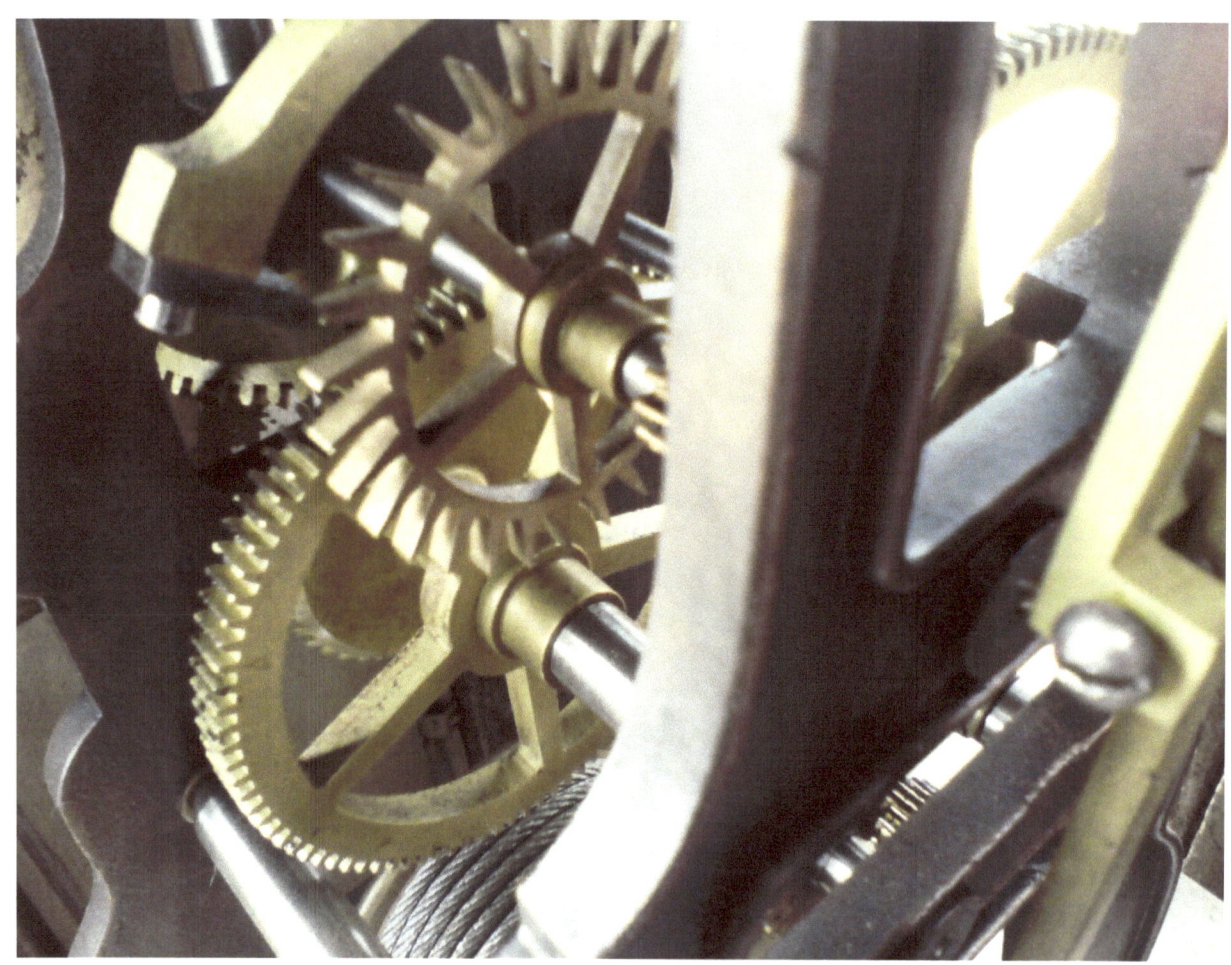

"Mechanical Precision" 2015

As we come to the wondrous clock with four sides that looks like some steampunk transplant from the eighteen hundreds. We inspect the glass display of the gears doing their precise calculations, when we are greeted by a friendly jeweler named Bruce Simpson. He tells us all about the wonderful history of the clock, as well as introducing us to the current owners; Allen and Jennifer Larsen. They are so committed to the clock that they manually wind it to keep it working. Then they opened the case so that we could get some better photographs of the gears, all the while going through its history and the shared history of these local merchants. The whole experience reminds us of why we are highlighting places just like these. The people are always friendly and more than willing to tell you all about their chosen piece of the world. While you may find that the experience is hard to let go of, you must wish your new friends well and continue upon the walk. It is hard to say goodbye to these wonderful new friends, but down a little north, the sounds of a waterfall can be heard.

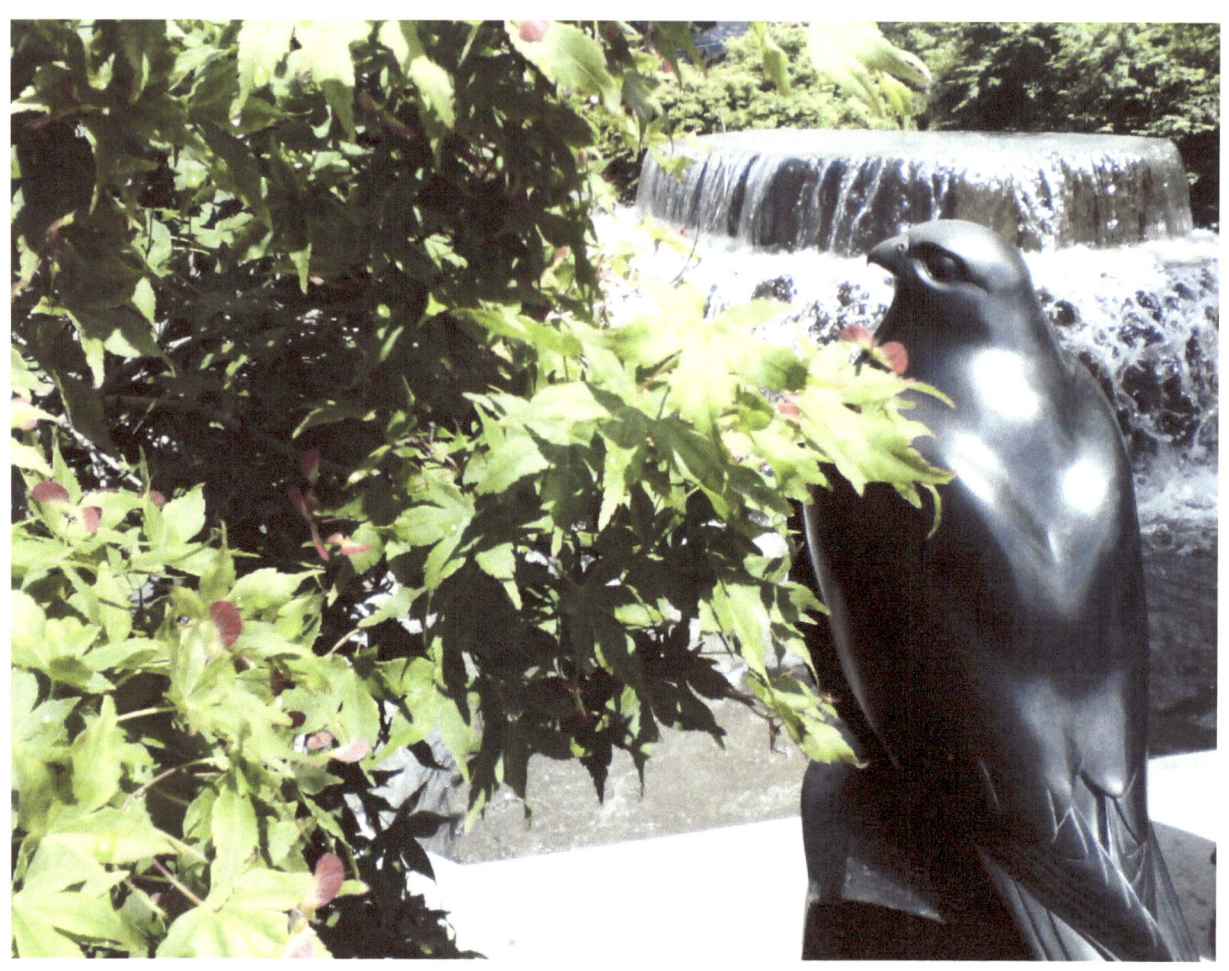

"Perfect on Petra" by Ross Matteson

As we make our way down the Avenue we come to the sound and surprisingly a strange bridge. Even though the day is winding down the sun is still quite hot, so a resting our weary bones at the waterfall seems more than appropriate. In the shade we find a partially hidden addition to the Art on the Avenues, a falcon that seems to be perpetually stalking the fountain for prey. Next to it we find our respite in the shade of the maples. With the flowing water and occasional spray of mist, this oasis seems like a serene spot from a mountain hike. Complete with the ever looming falcon's watchful eyes. It is easy to get kind of lost in this spot; with it's quite and straight out of nature feel. Yet in the back of my mind lies the nagging question of where does that strange bridge lead? So I guess we will bid our new area of Zen Aude. It's off to the mystery bridge with us and on with our journey!

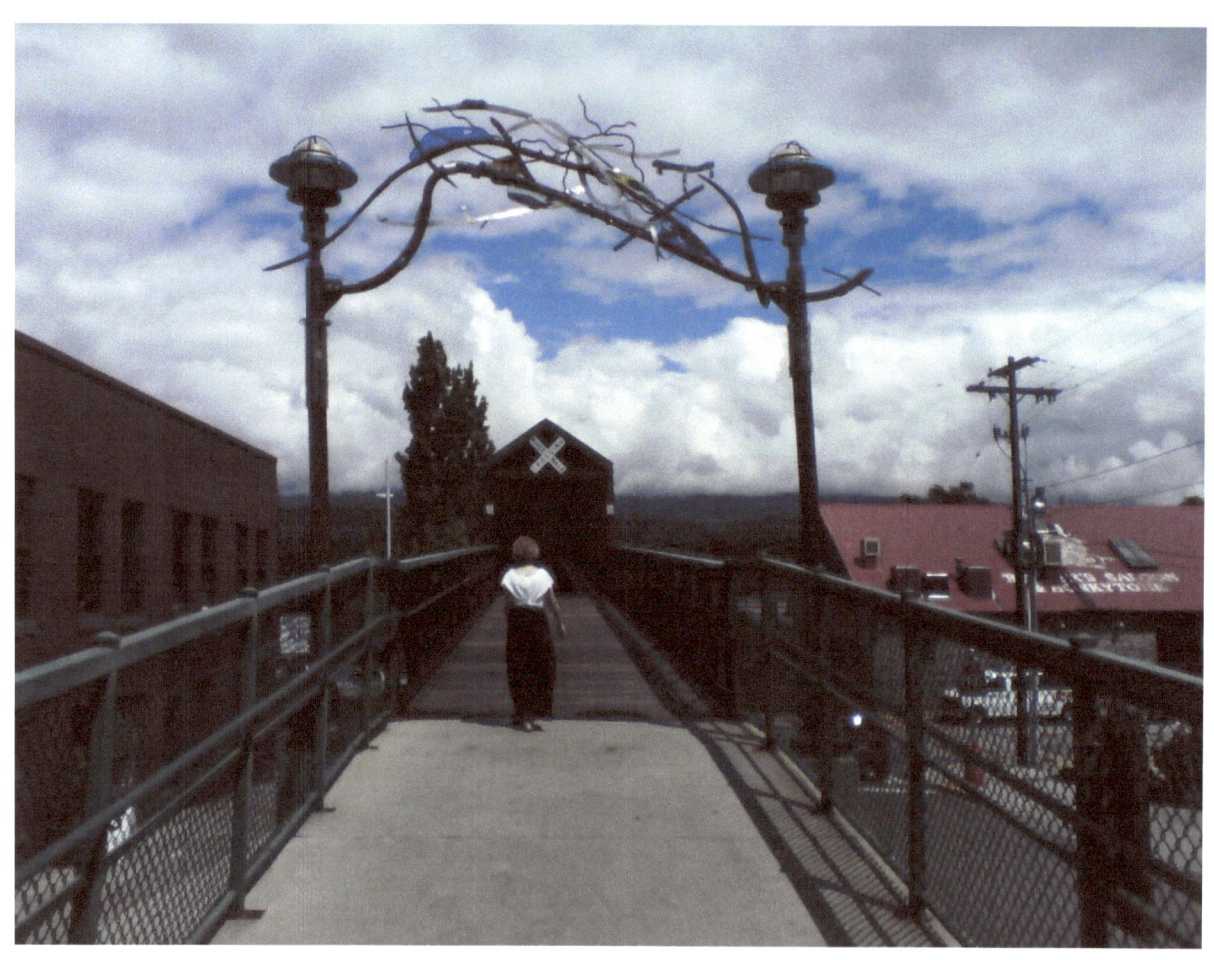

"The Bridge" 2015

My wife and I decided to take this journey and she even agreed to let me take her photo as we began.

As we pass under the strange archway, we are struck by the ways in which the lights of the day play

through the glass. It creates a feeling of intrigue and you are instantly transported to some magical

journey through the senses around you. That's not all that turns out to be striking, as this bridge

begins to rise over the nearby buildings, giving one a sense of being above it all. It then winds around

and over the railroad tracks. Then it lets you out of its surreal, transporting grip and into a serene park

filled with all kinds of sculptures for one to explore. However, we will have to explore these in the

next walk, as the light is waning and we still have to make it to the Pybus Market and the rest of the

waterfront. So on with the journey.

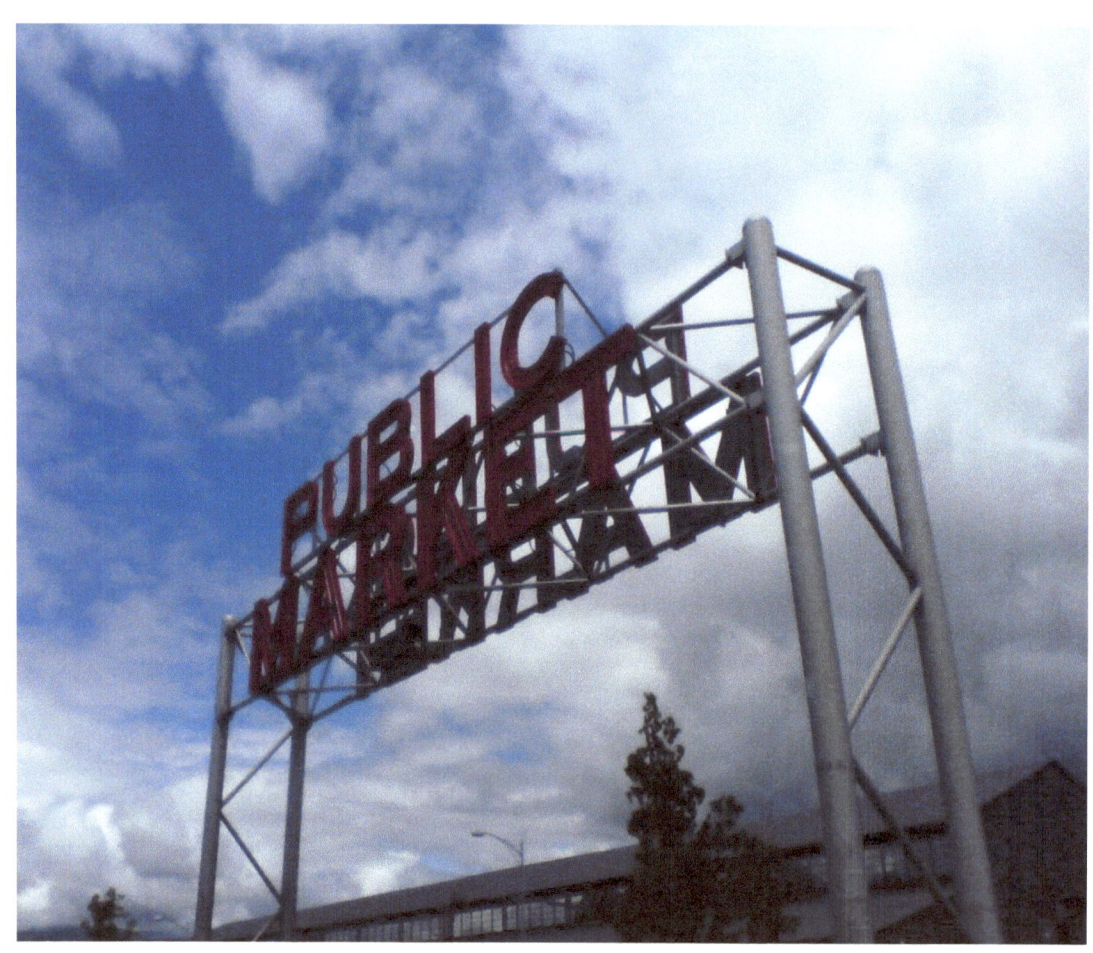

"The Pybus" 2015

As we head to the right of the trail it is but a small walk past the sculptures and near a boat ramp to the back side of the Pybus Public Market. Here we find ourselves once again amongst the bustling crowds of people. We are immediately struck with the competing aromas of bistros and cafes of all sorts. Looking like a transplant from Seattle, it hides its charm in the nondescript warehouse building, only giving away a little with the shiny Airstream selling delights at the edge of the parking lot and the South restaurant beckoning customers with their misting machines and aromatic scents. Once inside however, we are greeted by a varied group of vendors plying their crafts, some wooden toys for children and others canned concoctions. Of course the ever present fruit industry is also heavily represented here, by both local farmers and Auvil Fruit. A wonderful place to sit and enjoy some good ole fashioned people watching. There are also bicycle rentals for those intrepid few who wish to ride the entirety of the Apple Capital Loop Trail, a trail which does a loop around the entire interior of Wenatchee. Again, sadly we will not be able to do that on this walk, as we are rested and ready to end our journey near the great Columbia River.

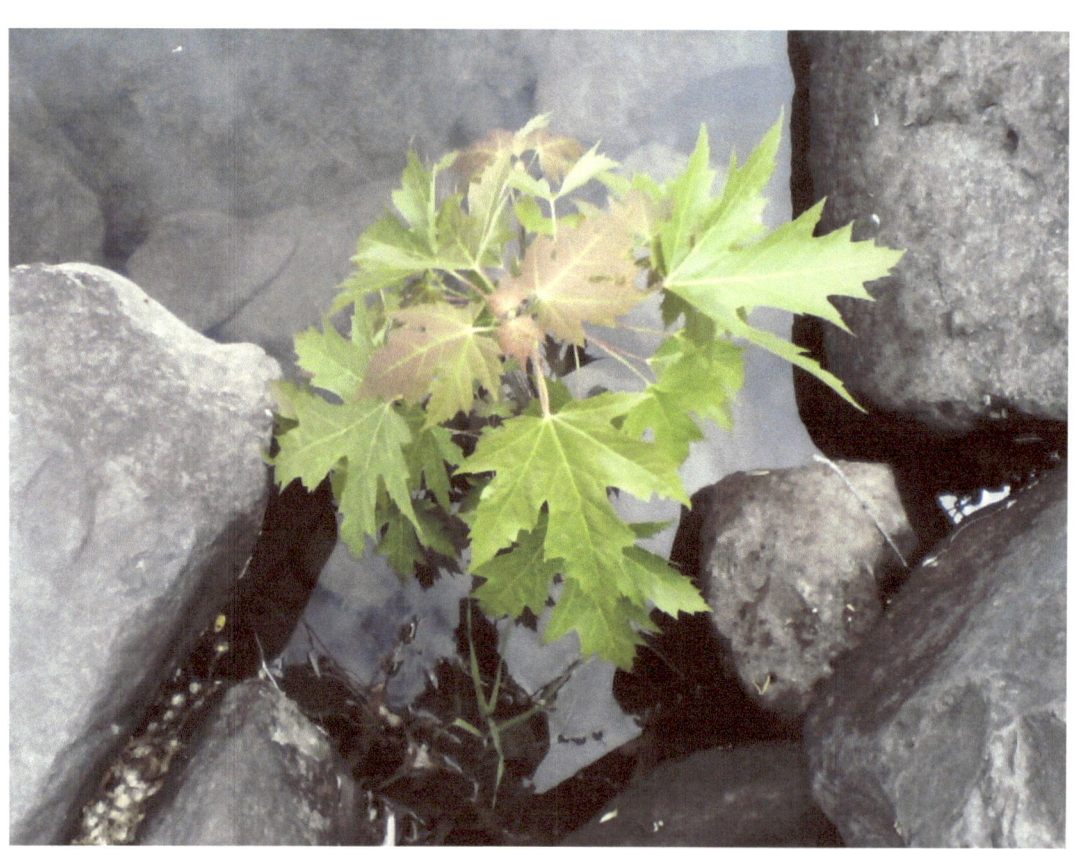

"Water Maple" 2015

Returning to our journey, we leave our new favorite market behind and travel through the back door once again. Crossing the parking areas and continuing past the boat launch we come to a little park where we are able to at last reach out to touch the great Columbia. Here our earlier pondering about the life of a poppy is renewed, when we find another of nature's survivors. As we approached the river we found a small jetty of rocks, where we could almost step out into the river. When out of the corner of the eye, I spotted this little maple sapling jutting out from the water, its roots tangled amongst the rocks below. I could not resist capturing it, as it sort of screamed out to be noticed, with its thirst for life exceeding its need for land. With this picture of tenacity fresh on our minds, we settle down to relax in the lush green grass of the park next the remarkable maple. Here we are greeted with a peaceful and serene setting, right in the middle of town. Glancing up from my view of this struggle for life, I saw the "old bridge as it's called.

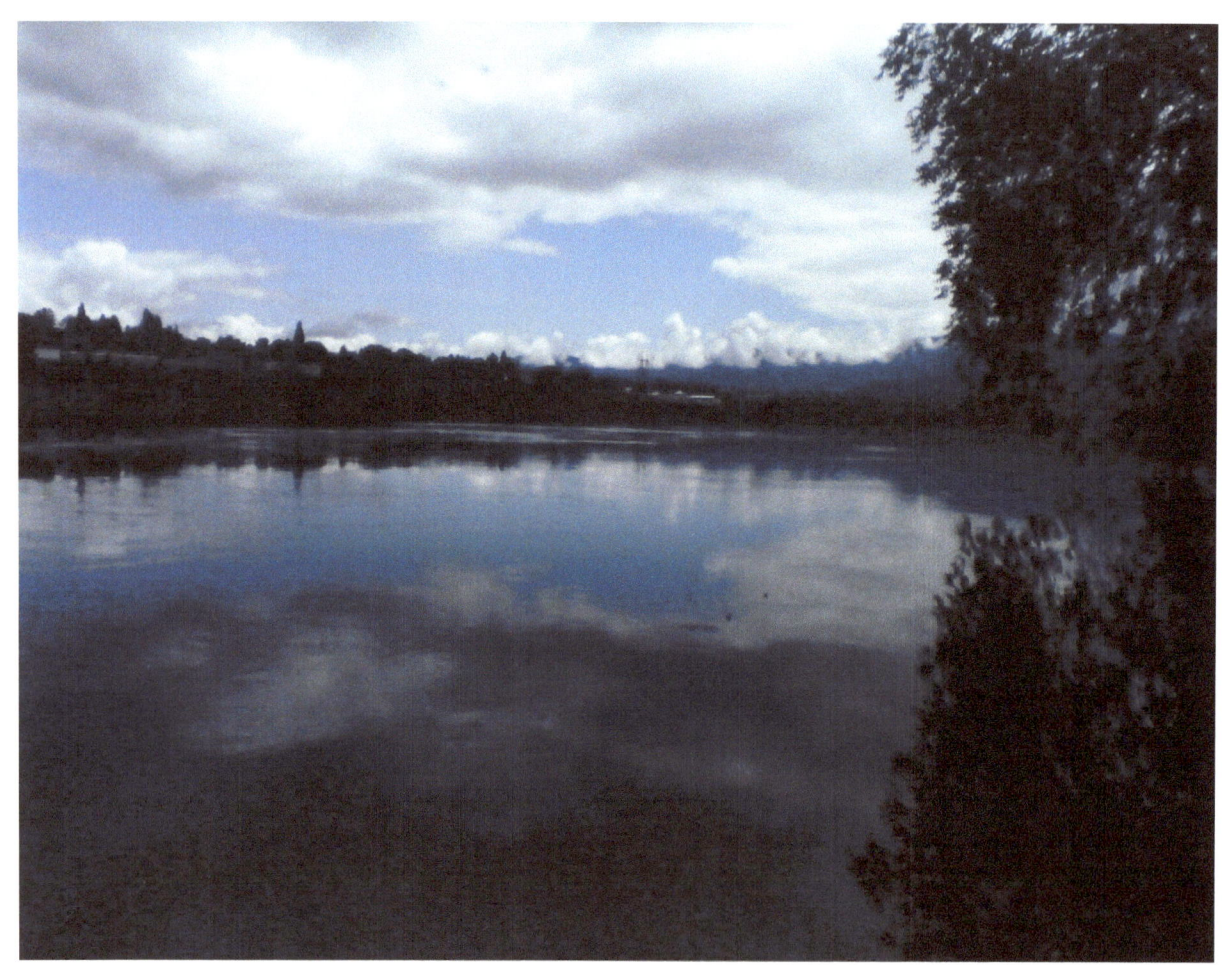

"Symmetric Serenity" 2015

Looking out towards the bridge of progress past, I find the perfect symmetrical scene, with clouds forming on both the mighty Columbia, as well in the great expanse above. Providing the perfect moment to capture the essence of the valley; a simple symmetry. It definitely has a calming effect on the soul. It also offers the perfect way to end our little journey through Wenatchee. So here we will part, having shared this more local view of a wonderful little city in the center of the Evergreen state.

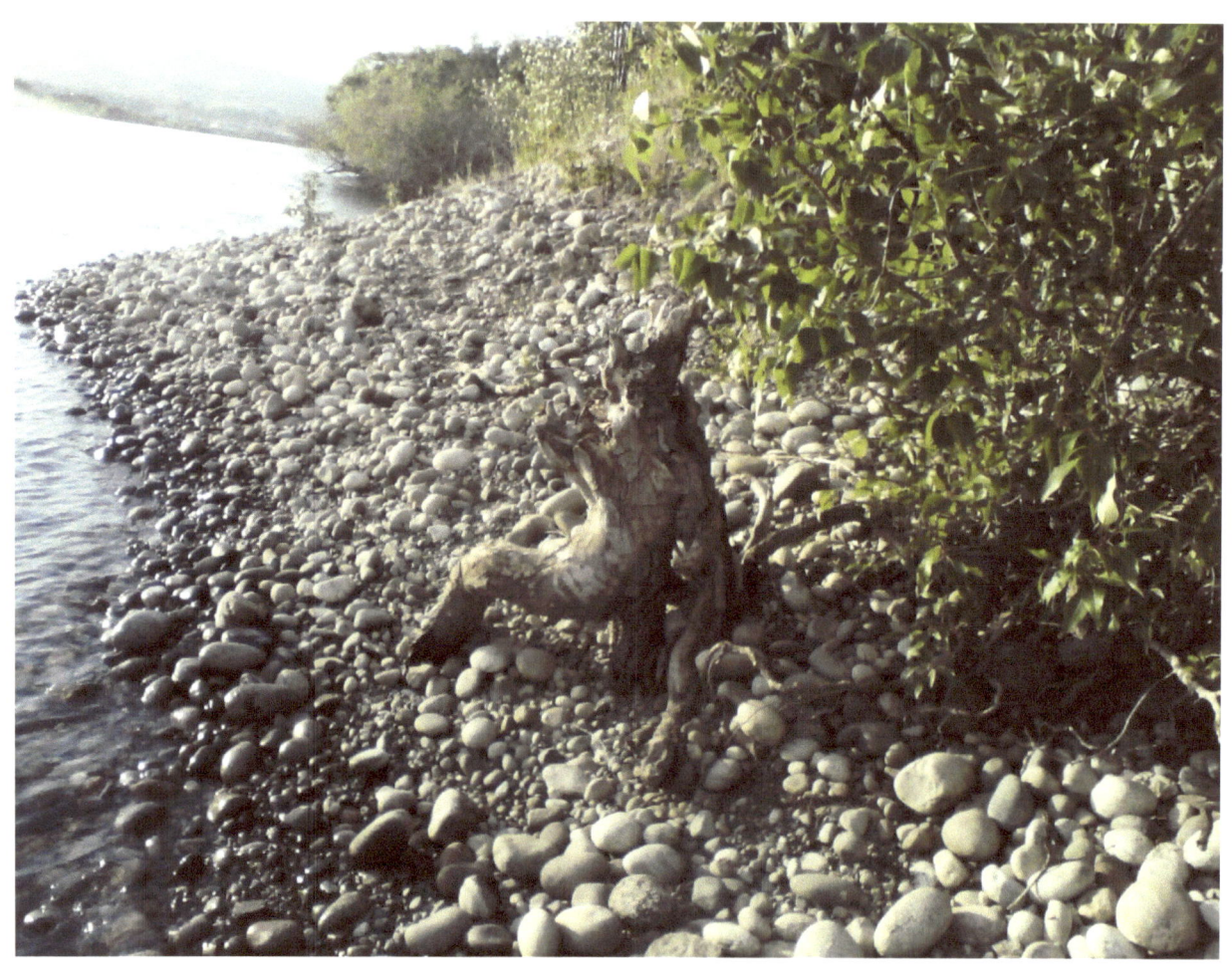

"Man of the river" 2015

So as we come to the end of our journey, I would like to leave you with the waving vision of a man who seemed to be made of the river himself. Thank you all for taking this journey with me and I hope you will join me for future journeys. I would also like to thank a number of groups and individuals who were gracious enough to give me permissions to publish much of this work.

The City of Wenatchee

Art on the Avenues and Adele Wolford

Appleatchee Riders

Pybus Market

Bruce Simpson

Allen and Jennifer Larsen.

Thank you to all of you!

Corey Oakes 2015

www.ingramcontent.com/pod-product-compliance
Lightning Source LLC
Chambersburg PA
CBHW050402180526
45159CB00005B/2116